Python

FOR BEGINNERS

The Comprehensive Guide To Learning, Understanding, And Mastering Python Programming

AF720347

PYTHON FOR BEGINNERS

The Comprehensive Guide To Learning, Understanding, And Mastering Python Programming

PYTHON FOR BEGINNERS: THE COMPREHENSIVE GUIDE TO LEARNING, UNDERSTANDING, AND MASTERING PYTHON PROGRAMMING

First edition. November 29, 2023.

Written by Voltaire Lumiere.

TABLE OF CONTENTS

INTRODUCTION

EMBARKING ON A PYTHON JOURNEY

Welcome to the captivating world of programming, where logic meets creativity, and possibilities unfold with each line of code. If you're holding this book, you've taken the first step into the realm of Python, a language revered for its simplicity, versatility, and the boundless opportunities it offers.

Unveiling the Python Tapestry:

"Python for Beginners" is not just a book; it's your passport to a realm where the syntax is friendly, the concepts are approachable, and the potential is limitless. Whether you're a curious novice eager to unravel the secrets of programming or someone transitioning from another language, Python is the perfect gateway.

Why Python?

Python's popularity transcends industries—from web development and data science to artificial intelligence and automation. Its readability, coupled with a vast standard library, makes it a language that can be wielded with ease by newcomers and seasoned developers alike. The beauty of Python lies in its simplicity, allowing you to focus on solving problems and bringing your ideas to life.

What Awaits You:

In the pages that follow, you'll embark on a journey structured to nurture your understanding of Python's fundamentals and guide you through progressively more complex concepts. From variables and data types to loops, functions, and object-oriented programming, each chapter unfolds a layer of Python's elegance.

Key Highlights:

1. **Hands-On Learning:**

- Brace yourself for a hands-on experience. The best way to learn programming is by doing, and you'll find ample exercises and examples to solidify your understanding.

2. **Real-World Applications:**

- Discover how Python is used in the real world. From web development frameworks like Django to data analysis with pandas, you'll explore applications that showcase Python's versatility.

3. **Problem-Solving Mindset:**

- Programming is a journey of problem-solving. As you advance, you'll develop a problem-solving mindset—a skill applicable not only in the world of coding but in various aspects of life.

4. **Community and Resources:**

- Join a vibrant global community of Python enthusiasts. Learn where to find resources, ask questions, and stay updated with the latest trends in the Python ecosystem.

Who Is This Book For?

This book is tailored for beginners—those taking their first steps into the coding universe. Whether you're a student exploring programming for the first time, a professional transitioning to a technical role, or someone simply intrigued by the art of code, you'll find a welcoming guide in these pages.

The Adventure Begins:

So, fasten your seatbelt and get ready to embark on a Pythonic adventure. "Python for Beginners" is not just a tutorial; it's your companion on a journey of exploration and mastery. Let the coding odyssey commence!

CHAPTER 1
PYTHON OVER THE HISTORY OF PROGRAMMING

A Brief History of Python

In this chapter, we'll explore the fascinating journey of Python from its humble beginnings to becoming one of the most popular programming languages in the world.

Birth of Python:

Python was conceived in the late 1980s by Guido van Rossum, a Dutch programmer working at the Centrum Wiskunde & Informatica (CWI) in the Netherlands. In December 1989, Guido began developing Python as a side project during his Christmas vacation, seeking to create a language that combined the best features of existing languages while addressing some of their limitations.

Python 0.9.0 and the "Python" Name:

Python's first version, Python 0.9.0, was released on February 20, 1991. This initial version already showcased essential features like classes with inheritance, exception handling, and functions. Guido chose the name "Python" inspired by his love for the British comedy television show "Monty Python's Flying Circus."

Python 1.0:

Python 1.0, released on January 26, 1994, marked a significant milestone in the language's development. The release solidified Python as a stable and usable programming language, gaining attention from developers around the world.

Python 2.x and 3.x: The Great Schism:

Over the years, Python continued to evolve with numerous improvements and enhancements. However, this evolution created a divide between the Python 2.x and 3.x versions, known as the "Python 2 versus Python 3" or "Python 2/3" debate. The release of Python 3.0 on December 3, 2008, introduced changes that were not backward compatible with Python 2.x, resulting in a transitional period for the community.

Python 3.x Adoption:

While the transition to Python 3.x posed challenges due to the existing codebase in Python 2.x, the Python community worked diligently to encourage adoption. The final Python 2 release, Python 2.7, was released on July 3, 2010, and received support until January 1, 2020. Many libraries and frameworks eventually migrated to Python 3, cementing its status as the future of the language.

Python's Popularity Soars:

In the early 2000s, Python's popularity soared, driven by its ease of use, versatility, and active community. Major companies, such as Google, YouTube, Dropbox, and Instagram, adopted Python as their language of choice for various projects, propelling its widespread adoption.

The Zen of Python:

"The Zen of Python" is a collection of guiding principles for Python's design, encapsulated in a series of aphorisms. These principles, often humorous yet profound, reflect the philosophy behind Python's simplicity, elegance, and readability.

Python Software Foundation (PSF):

In 2001, the Python Software Foundation (PSF) was established as a non-profit organization to promote, protect, and advance Python and its community. The PSF plays a crucial role in organizing Python conferences, funding development projects, and managing the intellectual property related to Python.

Python's Ongoing Evolution:

Python continues to evolve with regular updates and improvements. The community-driven Python Enhancement Proposal (PEP) process allows developers to propose and discuss new features or changes to the language.

From its inception as a personal project to its status as a ubiquitous and powerful programming language, Python's journey has been remarkable. Guido van Rossum's vision of creating a language that emphasizes simplicity and elegance has stood the test of time. Python's journey is far from over, and it remains a dynamic and influential force in the world of programming, attracting new developers and seasoned professionals alike to be a part of its ever-expanding community.

CHAPTER 2

APPLICATIONS OF PYTHON

In this chapter, we'll explore the vast array of applications that Python offers across different domains and industries. Python's versatility and rich ecosystem have made it a go-to language for a wide range of tasks and projects.

Web Development:

Python's simplicity and ease of use have resulted in the development of several popular web frameworks. Django, Flask, and Pyramid are some of the frameworks that have gained significant traction. These frameworks empower developers to build robust and scalable web applications efficiently. Python's web development capabilities have been utilized by companies like Instagram, Pinterest, and Mozilla.

Data Science and Machine Learning:

Python's libraries, such as NumPy, Pandas, and Scikit-learn, have solidified its position as a dominant player in the data science and machine learning domains. With Python, data analysts and scientists can perform data manipulation, analysis, and visualization. Additionally, Python's integration with popular machine learning libraries allows developers to build complex predictive models for various applications.

Scientific Computing:

Python's capabilities in scientific computing have made it an attractive choice for researchers and scientists. Libraries like SciPy, SymPy, and Matplotlib provide the tools necessary for numerical computing, symbolic mathematics, and data visualization in scientific research and engineering.

Automation and Scripting:

Python's ease of use and platform independence make it an excellent choice for automating repetitive tasks and writing system scripts. Whether it's automating file operations, data processing, or network communication, Python's simplicity facilitates the creation of efficient scripts.

Artificial Intelligence and Natural Language Processing:

Python has emerged as a popular language for artificial intelligence and natural language processing (NLP) applications. Libraries like TensorFlow, Keras, and NLTK (Natural Language Toolkit) enable developers to create sophisticated AI models, including neural networks and language processing algorithms.

Game Development:

Python is also finding its place in the realm of game development. The Pygame library, built on top of the Simple DirectMedia Layer (SDL), provides an easy-to-use platform for creating 2D games. While not as performant as some other languages like C++, Python's rapid development capabilities make it an attractive choice for smaller game projects and prototypes.

Internet of Things (IoT):

Python's lightweight nature and versatility make it a suitable choice for Internet of Things (IoT) projects. With libraries like Raspberry Pi GPIO and CircuitPython, developers can interface with sensors, devices, and IoT platforms, enabling them to build smart and connected solutions.

Scripting for Software and System Administration:

Python is widely used for scripting tasks related to software and system administration. System administrators use Python scripts to automate server maintenance, manage databases, and deploy applications, saving time and reducing human error.

Desktop GUI Applications:

Python can be used to create desktop Graphical User Interface (GUI) applications with libraries like Tkinter, PyQt, and wxPython.

These libraries provide a platform-independent way to design and develop desktop applications with graphical interfaces.

The applications of Python are as diverse as the interests and needs of developers and businesses. Its flexibility, ease of use, and large community support have contributed to its success in various domains, making it an indispensable tool for projects ranging from web development to data science, artificial intelligence, automation, and much more. Python's journey as a versatile and powerful language is ongoing, and its widespread adoption continues to shape the future of technology and innovation.

Different Versions of Python

As Python has evolved over the years, several major versions have been released, each introducing new features and improvements. As of my last update in September 2021, the following are the significant versions of Python:

Python 1.x Series:

- Python 1.0 (January 26, 1994): The first official release of Python, laying the foundation for the language's growth.

Python 2.x Series:

- Python 2.0 (October 16, 2000): Introduced list comprehensions, garbage collection improvements, and other enhancements.

- Python 2.7 (July 3, 2010): The final release in the Python 2.x series. It provided support for several years to facilitate the transition to Python 3.

Python 3.x Series:

- Python 3.0 (December 3, 2008): A major release that introduced several backward-incompatible changes to improve the language's design and remove redundant features. It marked the beginning of the Python 3.x series.
- Python 3.5 (September 13, 2015): Introduced "async" and "await" keywords for asynchronous programming support, and also improved type hinting capabilities.
- Python 3.6 (December 23, 2016): Introduced f-strings for more concise string formatting, "asyncio" enhancements, and dictionary ordering preservation.
- Python 3.7 (June 27, 2018): Added various performance optimizations, including faster built-in functions and dictionary improvements.
- Python 3.8 (October 14, 2019): Introduced the "walrus operator" (:=), "position-only parameters," and more improvements to the "asyncio" module.

- Python 3.9 (October 5, 2020): Brought enhancements such as dictionary merging with the "update()" method, new syntax features, and type hinting improvements.
- Python 3.10 (Expected in October 2021): Anticipated to bring various new features, optimizations, and improvements, including structural pattern matching and new string methods.

Each new version of Python aims to enhance the language's capabilities, performance, and developer experience. With Python 2.x officially reaching the end of its support on January 1, 2020, it is recommended that developers and users migrate to Python 3.x for ongoing support and access to the latest features and improvements.

Setting Up Python

Setting up Python is a simple process, and there are different ways to do it depending on your operating system. Below are the general steps to set up Python on Windows, macOS, and Linux:

1. Check if Python is Already Installed:

Before you start the setup process, check if Python is already installed on your computer. Open a terminal or command prompt and type the following command:

python –version

If Python is installed, it will display the version number (e.g., Python 3.8.5). If not, you can proceed with the installation.

2. Windows:

- Visit the official Python website (https://www.python.org/downloads/windows/) and download the latest Python installer for Windows.
- Run the downloaded installer.
- Check the box "Add Python x.x to PATH" during the installation to make Python accessible from the command prompt.
- Click "Install Now" to begin the installation process.
- Once the installation is complete, open the command prompt and verify the Python installation by typing:

```
python –version
```

3. macOS:

- macOS typically comes with a pre-installed version of Python. However, it's recommended to install Python using Homebrew, a popular package manager for macOS.
- Open the Terminal application.
- Install Homebrew by following the instructions on the Homebrew website (https://brew.sh/).
- After installing Homebrew, use it to install Python by typing the following command in the Terminal:

```
brew install python
```

To verify the Python installation, type:

python3 –version

4. Linux:

- Most Linux distributions come with Python pre-installed. However, you can install it using the package manager specific to your distribution. For example:

- Ubuntu/Debian:

sudo apt-get update

sudo apt-get install python3

Fedora:

sudo dnf install python3

CentOS/RHEL:

sudo yum install python3

To verify the Python installation, type:

python3 –version

Note: In the commands above, "python" refers to Python 2.x, and "python3" refers to Python 3.x. For Python 3.x, you should always use "python3" to ensure you are using the correct version.

Congratulations! You have successfully set up Python on your system. Now you're ready to start writing Python code and exploring the vast world of programming with Python.

Getting Started with PyCharm and IDLE

PyCharm is a popular Integrated Development Environment (IDE) specifically designed for Python development. It provides a comprehensive set of tools for writing, debugging, and running Python code efficiently. Here's how you can get started with PyCharm:

1. **Install PyCharm:**

- Go to the JetBrains website (https://www.jetbrains.com/pycharm/) and download the appropriate version of PyCharm for your operating system (Community Edition is free and suitable for most Python projects).
- Run the downloaded installer and follow the on-screen instructions to install PyCharm.

2. **Create a New Project:**

- Launch PyCharm after installation.
- Click on "Create New Project" to start a new Python project.
- Choose the project location, interpreter (select the Python version you installed earlier), and click "Create."

3. **Write and Run Code:**

- PyCharm will open a new Python file where you can start writing your code.

- To run your code, right-click inside the editor and select "Run <your_filename.py>" or use the green play button in the top right corner.
- PyCharm will execute your Python script and display the output in the Run tool window.

4. **Debugging:**

- PyCharm provides a powerful debugging feature to help you identify and fix issues in your code.
- To set breakpoints, click in the left gutter of the editor next to the line of code where you want to pause the execution.
- Click the "Debug" button or right-click and select "Debug <your_filename.py>" to run your code in debug mode. The execution will pause at breakpoints, allowing you to inspect variables and step through your code line by line.

5. **Code Assistance and Auto-Completion:**

- PyCharm offers intelligent code assistance, including auto-completion, code navigation, and code refactoring suggestions, making your development process more efficient.

Getting Started with IDLE:

IDLE (Integrated Development and Learning Environment) is a simple Python IDE that comes bundled with the standard Python installation. It provides a basic set of features for writing and running Python code. Here's how you can get started with IDLE:

1. **Open IDLE:**

- If you're using Windows, you can open IDLE by searching for "IDLE" in the Start menu.
- On macOS or Linux, you can typically open IDLE from the applications menu.

2. **Create a New Python File:**

- Once IDLE is open, click on "File" and then "New File" to create a new Python file.
- Write your Python code in the editor.

3. **Run Code:**

- To run your code, click on "Run" in the menu and then select "Run Module" or use the F5 key.
- IDLE will execute your Python script and display the output in the Python Shell window.

4. **Debugging:**

- Unlike PyCharm, IDLE does not offer advanced debugging features. For debugging, you may need to use print statements or other basic debugging techniques.

5. **Code Assistance:**

- IDLE provides basic code assistance, such as syntax highlighting and indentation guides.

Both PyCharm and IDLE have their advantages, and the choice between them depends on your preferences and project requirements. PyCharm is more feature-rich and suitable for professional development, while IDLE is lightweight and sufficient for simple projects and learning Python basics.

CHAPTER 3
PYTHON STYLE GUIDE

A Python Style Guide, also known as PEP 8 (Python Enhancement Proposal 8), is a set of guidelines and conventions for writing clean, readable, and maintainable Python code. It is highly recommended to follow PEP 8 to ensure consistency and readability in your Python projects, especially when collaborating with other developers. Here are some key points from PEP 8:

1. **Indentation:**

- Use 4 spaces for each level of indentation. Avoid using tabs.
- Be consistent with indentation throughout the codebase.

2. **Line Length:**

- Limit lines to a maximum of 79 characters. If necessary, you can extend to 99 characters for comments or docstrings.
- Break long lines using parentheses or backslashes, and prefer vertical alignment for multiple function arguments.

3. **Whitespace:**

- Use a single space after commas, colons, and semicolons. Avoid any whitespace before these punctuation marks.
- Avoid extraneous whitespace at the beginning or end of lines.

4. **Blank Lines:**

- Use blank lines sparingly to separate logical sections of code and improve readability.
- Use two blank lines before class and function definitions.

5. **Imports:**

- Imports should be grouped in the following order:
    - Standard library imports
    - Third-party library imports
    - Local application imports
- Each group should be separated by a blank line.

6. **Naming Conventions:**

- Use descriptive variable and function names, preferably in lowercase, with words separated by underscores (snake_case).
- Class names should use CamelCase.

- Constants should be in uppercase with words separated by underscores.

7. **Comments and Docstrings:**

- Write comments to explain non-obvious code or clarify complex logic.
- Use docstrings to document functions, classes, and modules. Follow the conventions of the "docstring conventions" section in PEP 257.

8. **Function and Method Arguments:**

- Be consistent with the naming of function and method arguments.
- Avoid using single-character variable names for function arguments unless they have a clear meaning.

9. **Boolean Expressions:**

- Use explicit comparisons (e.g., **if x is None** instead of **if x**).
- Avoid unnecessary parentheses in boolean expressions.

10. **Exception Handling:**

- Only catch specific exceptions, not the general **Exception**.

- Limit the use of bare **except:** statements. Specify the exception(s) you want to catch explicitly.

Remember that adherence to PEP 8 is not mandatory, but it is highly recommended to foster code consistency and maintainability across Python projects. Consistency is essential when collaborating with other developers, as it allows everyone to understand and maintain the code more efficiently.

CHAPTER 4

INPUT AND OUTPUT IN PYTHON

Input and output (I/O) in Python allows you to interact with the user and read/write data to and from files or other external sources. Python provides built-in functions and methods for performing these tasks. Here's an overview of input and output in Python:

Input:

Reading User Input:

To read input from the user, you can use the **input()** function. It takes an optional prompt as an argument and returns the user's input as a string. For example:

```
name = input("Enter your name: ")

print("Hello, " + name)
```

Output:

Printing to the Console:

To display output on the console, you can use the **print()** function. It takes one or more arguments and prints them to the console, separated by spaces by default. For example:

```
print("Hello, World!")
```

Formatted Output:

You can use string formatting to create more complex output. Python provides several methods for formatting strings, such as using **%** operator or **str.format()**. However, the recommended way is to use f-strings (formatted string literals) available in Python 3.6 and above. For example:

```
name = "John"

age = 30

print(f"My name is {name} and I am {age} years old.")
```

File I/O:

Opening and Closing Files:

To work with files, you need to open them first using the **open()** function. It takes the file path and the mode (e.g., **'r'** for reading, **'w'** for writing, **'a'** for appending) as arguments. After performing the necessary operations, it's essential to close the file using the **close()** method. However, a more recommended approach is to use a context manager (**with** statement) to ensure the file is automatically closed when done. For example:

```
with open('file.txt', 'r') as file:

  content = file.read()
```

Reading from Files:

To read the contents of a file, you can use methods like **read()** to read the entire file, **readline()** to read a single line, or **readlines()** to read all lines as a list. For example:

```
with open('file.txt', 'r') as file:
  content = file.read()      # Reads the entire file as a single string
  line = file.readline()     # Reads the first line of the file
  lines = file.readlines()    # Reads all lines of the file as a list of strings
```

Writing to Files:

To write data to a file, you can use the **write()** method. It writes the specified string to the file. For example:

```
with open('output.txt', 'w') as file:
  file.write("This is a sample output.")
```

Remember to handle exceptions when performing file I/O, as file operations can raise errors, such as **FileNotFoundError** or **PermissionError**. Always close files properly after using them to prevent resource leaks.

Comments, Reserved Keywords, and Operators

Comments in Python are used to add explanatory notes within the code that are ignored by the interpreter during execution. They help make the code more readable and provide insights into the code's functionality. In Python, comments are denoted using the # symbol. Anything after the # on the same line is considered a comment. For example:

```
# This is a single-line comment

print("Hello, World!")  # This is also a comment
```

You can also create multi-line comments using triple quotes (either single or double). While these triple quotes are primarily used to create docstrings for functions, they can also serve as multi-line comments:

```
"""

This is a multi-line comment.

It spans multiple lines and can be used for longer explanations.

"""
```

Reserved Keywords in Python:

Reserved keywords in Python are words that have predefined meanings and are part of the language syntax. They cannot be used as variable names or identifiers, as they serve specific purposes in Python. Here are some examples of reserved keywords in Python:

and as assert break class continue def

del elif else except False finally for

from global if import in is lambda

None nonlocal not or pass raise return

True try while with yield

Operators in Python:

Operators in Python are symbols or special keywords used to perform operations on variables, values, or expressions. Python supports a wide range of operators, including:

1. **Arithmetic Operators:**

- + (addition)
- - (subtraction)
- * (multiplication)
- / (division)
- % (modulus - remainder of division)
- ** (exponentiation)
- // (floor division - division with the result rounded down to the nearest integer)

2. **Comparison Operators:**

- == (equal to)
- != (not equal to)

- > (greater than)
- < (less than)
- >= (greater than or equal to)
- <= (less than or equal to)

3. **Logical Operators:**

- **and** (logical AND)
- **or** (logical OR)
- **not** (logical NOT)

4. **Assignment Operators:**

- = (simple assignment)
- += (increment and assign)
- -= (decrement and assign)
- *= (multiply and assign)
- /= (divide and assign)
- %=, **=, //=, etc. (other assignment operators)

5. **Bitwise Operators:**

- **&** (bitwise AND)
- | (bitwise OR)
- ^ (bitwise XOR)

- ~ (bitwise NOT)
- << (left shift)
- >> (right shift)

6. **Membership Operators:**

- **in** (checks if a value exists in a sequence)
- **not in** (checks if a value does not exist in a sequence)

7. **Identity Operators:**

- **is** (checks if two variables refer to the same object)
- **is not** (checks if two variables refer to different objects)

These are some of the essential aspects of comments, reserved keywords, and operators in Python. Understanding these concepts is fundamental to writing clear and effective Python code.

CHAPTER 5

WOKING WITH VARIABLES

Understanding variables is essential in any programming language, including Python. Variables are used to store and manipulate data during the execution of a program. Here's a detailed explanation of variables in Python:

What is a Variable?

In Python, a variable is a name assigned to a memory location that holds a value. Variables act as containers for storing data, such as numbers, strings, lists, or more complex objects. They allow you to access and manipulate data throughout your program.

Variable Naming Rules:

- Variable names in Python can contain letters (a-z, A-Z), digits (0-9), and underscores (_).
- The first character of a variable name cannot be a digit; it must be a letter or an underscore.
- Variable names are case-sensitive, meaning **my_variable** and **My_Variable** are different variables.
- Avoid using Python's reserved keywords as variable names.

Declaring and Assigning Values to Variables:

In Python, you can declare a variable and assign a value to it using the assignment operator (=). For example:

```
age = 25

name = "John Doe"

is_student = True
```

Here, we have created three variables: **age**, **name**, and **is_student**. **age** stores an integer value, **name** stores a string value, and **is_student** stores a Boolean value.

Variable Types in Python:

Python is a dynamically typed language, which means you don't need to declare the data type of a variable explicitly. Python automatically determines the data type based on the assigned value. Common variable types in Python include:

- Numeric Types: **int** (integer), **float** (floating-point number), and **complex** (complex number).
- Sequence Types: **str** (string), **list** (list), **tuple** (tuple).
- Boolean Type: **bool** (Boolean, either **True** or **False**).
- Other Types: **dict** (dictionary), **set** (set), **NoneType** (None).

Variable Reassignment:

In Python, you can change the value of a variable by assigning it a new value:

```
x = 10
print(x)  # Output: 10
x = 20
print(x)  # Output: 20
```

The variable **x** is first assigned the value **10**, and later it is reassigned the value **20**.

Variable Scope:

Variables have a scope that defines where they can be accessed. In Python, variables can have either a global scope (accessible throughout the program) or a local scope (accessible only within a specific block of code, such as a function).

```
# Global variable
x = 100
def my_function():
  # Local variable
  y = 50
  print(x)  # Accessing the global variable
  print(y)  # Accessing the local variable
my_function()
print(x)      # Output: 100
```

print(y)   # This will raise an error since y is a local variable within my_function

In the example above, **x** is a global variable that can be accessed both inside and outside the function **my_function**. However, **y** is a local variable that can only be accessed within **my_function**.

Understanding variables is fundamental to writing effective Python code. They allow you to store data and work with it in a flexible and dynamic manner.

Naming and Defining Variables

Naming and defining variables is a crucial aspect of writing clean and maintainable code in Python. Choosing meaningful and descriptive names for variables enhances code readability and makes it easier for others to understand your code. Here are some guidelines for naming and defining variables in Python:

1. Variable Naming Rules:

- Variable names must start with a letter (a-z, A-Z) or an underscore (_).
- After the first character, variable names can include letters, digits (0-9), and underscores.
- Variable names are case-sensitive, so **my_variable** and **My_Variable** are different variables.

- Avoid using Python's reserved keywords as variable names, as they have predefined meanings.

2. Choosing Descriptive Names:

- Use meaningful and descriptive names that convey the purpose of the variable.
- Choose variable names that make the code self-explanatory and easy to understand.

3. Camel Case vs. Snake Case:

- Python programmers generally follow two conventions for multi-word variable names: camel case and snake case.
- Camel Case: Capitalize the first letter of each word, except the first word. For example: **firstName**, **lastName**.
- Snake Case: Use all lowercase letters and separate words with underscores. For example: **first_name**, **last_name**.

4. Avoid Using Single Characters:

- Avoid using single-character variable names (e.g., **x**, **y**, **i**) unless they represent loop counters in short loops.
- Use descriptive names even for temporary variables to improve code readability.

5. Avoid Ambiguous Abbreviations:

- Avoid using cryptic or ambiguous abbreviations that might confuse other developers. Instead, choose descriptive names.

- For example, use **customer_id** instead of **cid**, **counter** instead of **cnt**, and so on.

6. Defining Variables:

- Variables in Python are defined using the assignment operator (=).

- You don't need to explicitly declare the data type of a variable; Python infers it based on the assigned value.

Examples:

Here are some examples of well-named and defined variables:

```
# Good examples

first_name = "John"

last_name = "Doe"

age = 30

is_student = True

total_amount = 100.50

user_list = ["Alice", "Bob", "Carol"]

# Avoid using single-character or ambiguous names
```

```python
x = 10        # Instead, use something like 'counter' or 'num_of_students'

# Avoid ambiguous abbreviations
cid = 123   # Instead, use 'customer_id'
```

By following these guidelines, you can make your Python code more readable and maintainable. Naming and defining variables thoughtfully can significantly improve the overall quality of your codebase and help others understand your intentions clearly.

CHAPTER 6

MEMORY MANAGEMENT IN PYTHON

Memory management in Python is the process of efficiently allocating and releasing memory for objects during the execution of a program. Python uses a combination of techniques, including automatic garbage collection and reference counting, to manage memory effectively. Here's a brief overview of memory management in Python:

1. Reference Counting:

- Python uses reference counting as one of its memory management techniques. Every object in Python has a reference count that keeps track of the number of references to that object.
- When a new reference to an object is created (e.g., by assigning a variable to that object), Python increments the reference count. When a reference is removed or goes out of scope, Python decrements the reference count.
- When the reference count of an object becomes zero, meaning there are no references to that object, Python automatically deallocates the memory occupied by that object through garbage collection.

2. Garbage Collection:

- Garbage collection is the process of reclaiming memory occupied by objects that are no longer in use.
- In addition to reference counting, Python also uses a cyclic garbage collector to identify and collect objects with circular references (objects referencing each other in a loop), which are not reachable through reference counting alone.
- Python's garbage collector runs periodically and automatically deallocates memory for unused objects, freeing up resources for other purposes.

3. Memory Allocation and Deallocation:

- Python's memory manager handles the allocation and deallocation of memory for objects dynamically.
- When you create a new object (e.g., using **new_object = SomeClass()**), Python dynamically allocates memory for that object.
- When an object is no longer in use or goes out of scope, Python's memory manager deallocates the memory occupied by that object.

4. Memory Efficiency:

- Python's memory management allows it to efficiently use memory by deallocating unused objects promptly.

- The memory management system ensures that memory is released automatically, reducing the need for manual memory management and avoiding memory leaks.

5. Global Interpreter Lock (GIL):

- The Global Interpreter Lock (GIL) is a mechanism in CPython (the standard Python implementation) that ensures only one thread executes Python bytecode at a time.
- While the GIL simplifies memory management and makes Python memory-safe, it can also limit the performance of multi-threaded programs for CPU-bound tasks.

Memory Profiling:

- Python provides tools and libraries for memory profiling, allowing developers to analyze the memory usage of their programs and identify potential memory leaks or inefficiencies.

While Python's memory management is efficient and generally transparent to developers, it's essential to be aware of memory-intensive operations and circular references that may affect the program's performance and memory usage. Proper memory management practices, such as releasing unnecessary references and avoiding circular references, can help ensure optimal memory usage in Python programs.

Data Types in Python

In Python, data types define the type of data that can be stored in a variable. Python is a dynamically typed language, which means you don't need to declare the data type of a variable explicitly; Python infers the data type based on the assigned value. Here are some of thc common data types in Python:

1. Numeric Types:

- **int**: Integer data type, representing whole numbers (e.g., 1, -10, 100).
- **float**: Floating-point data type, representing decimal numbers (e.g., 3.14, -0.5, 2.0).

2. String Type:

- **str**: String data type, representing sequences of characters (e.g., "hello", 'world').

3. Boolean Type:

- **bool**: Boolean data type, representing either **True** or **False**.

4. Sequence Types:

- **list**: List data type, representing an ordered collection of elements that can be of different data types (e.g., [1, 2, 3], ['apple', 'banana']).

- **tuple**: Tuple data type, similar to a list, but immutable (cannot be changed after creation) (e.g., (1, 2, 3)).
- **range**: Range data type, representing an immutable sequence of numbers (e.g., range(0, 10)).

5. Set Types:

- **set**: Set data type, representing an unordered collection of unique elements (e.g., {1, 2, 3}).

6. Mapping Type:

- **dict**: Dictionary data type, representing a collection of key-value pairs (e.g., {'name': 'John', 'age': 30}).

7. None Type:

- **NoneType**: Represents the absence of a value. It is often used as a default return value for functions that don't explicitly return anything.

8. Custom Types:

- Python also allows you to define your own custom data types using classes. This allows you to create complex data structures and objects tailored to your specific needs.

Type Conversion (Type Casting):

- Python provides functions to convert one data type to another. For example, you can convert an integer to a string using the **str()** function or a string to an integer using the **int()** function.

For example:

```
# Type conversion example

x = 10

y = "20"

# Convert y from string to integer and perform addition

result = x + int(y)

print(result)  # Output: 30
```

Checking Data Types:

- You can check the data type of a variable using the **type()** function.

```
x = 10

y = "hello"

print(type(x))  # Output: <class 'int'>

print(type(y))  # Output: <class 'str'>
```

Python's dynamic typing allows for flexibility and simplicity in coding, but it's essential to be aware of data types, especially when performing operations that might result in unexpected behavior due to implicit type conversions.

Strings and String Manipulation

Strings are sequences of characters and represent text data in Python. They are one of the most commonly used data types, and Python provides various methods for string manipulation. Here are some common string operations and manipulation techniques:

1. Creating Strings:

- Strings can be created using single quotes (''), double quotes (""), or triple quotes (""") for multiline strings.

```
name1 = 'Alice'

name2 = "Bob"

multiline_string = """This is a

multiline string."""
```

2. Accessing Characters:

- You can access individual characters in a string using indexing.

```
text = "Hello, World!"

print(text[0])  # Output: 'H'

print(text[-1]) # Output: '!'
```

3. String Slicing:

- String slicing allows you to extract a substring from a larger string.

```
text = "Python Programming"

print(text[0:6])  # Output: 'Python'

print(text[7:])   # Output: 'Programming'

print(text[:6])   # Output: 'Python'
```

4. String Concatenation:

- You can concatenate (combine) strings using the + operator.

```
first_name = "John"

last_name = "Doe"

full_name = first_name + " " + last_name

print(full_name)  # Output: 'John Doe'
```

5. String Length:

- To get the length of a string, use the **len()** function.

```
text = "Hello, World!"

length = len(text)

print(length)  # Output: 13
```

6. String Methods:

- Python provides several built-in methods for string manipulation, such as **upper()**, **lower()**, **replace()**, **split()**, **strip()**, and more.

```
text = "Hello, World!"

print(text.upper())    # Output: 'HELLO, WORLD!'

print(text.lower())    # Output: 'hello, world!'

print(text.replace('l', 'L'))  # Output: 'HeLLo, WorLd!'

print(text.split(','))  # Output: ['Hello', ' World!']

print(text.strip())    # Output: 'Hello, World!'
```

7. String Formatting:

- String formatting allows you to embed variables or expressions inside a string.

```
name = "Alice"

age = 30

message = f"My name is {name} and I am {age} years old."

print(message)   # Output: 'My name is Alice and I am 30 years old.'
```

8. Escape Sequences:

- Use escape sequences to include special characters within strings.

```
text = "This is a \"quote\""

print(text)  # Output: 'This is a "quote"'
```

Strings in Python are immutable, meaning you cannot change individual characters within a string directly. However, you can create new strings with desired modifications using various string manipulation techniques. Understanding string manipulation is crucial for working with text data and processing user input in Python programs.

Numbers: Integers and Floating-Point

In Python, numbers are divided into two main types: integers and floating-point numbers.

Integers: Integers are whole numbers without any fractional part. They can be positive or negative. In Python, integers are represented using the **int** data type. Here are some examples of integers:

```
x = 10

y = -5

z = 0
```

Floating-Point Numbers: Floating-point numbers, or simply floats, are numbers with decimal points. They can also be expressed in scientific notation using the e or E notation. In Python, floating-point numbers are represented using the float data type. Here are some examples of floating-point numbers:

```
a = 3.14
b = -0.5
c = 2.0
d = 1.23e-4  # Equivalent to 0.000123
```

Operations with Numbers: Python supports various arithmetic operations for working with numbers. Here are some common arithmetic operations:

```
# Addition
sum_result = 5 + 3   # Output: 8
# Subtraction
difference = 10 - 3  # Output: 7
# Multiplication
product = 2 * 4      # Output: 8
# Division (returns a float)
division_result = 10 / 3  # Output: 3.3333333333333335
# Integer Division (returns an integer)
integer_division_result = 10 // 3  # Output: 3
# Modulus (returns the remainder)
```

```
remainder = 10 % 3   # Output: 1

# Exponentiation

power = 2 ** 3       # Output: 8
```

Type Conversion (Type Casting): Python allows you to convert numbers from one type to another using type casting. For example:

```
x = 10

y = 3.14

# Convert x to a float

x_float = float(x)  # Output: 10.0

# Convert y to an integer

y_int = int(y)      # Output: 3
```

When performing arithmetic operations between integers and floating-point numbers, Python automatically promotes the result to a floating-point number.

```
result = 5 + 3.14   # Output: 8.14
```

It's important to be aware of potential rounding errors with floating-point arithmetic due to the limited precision of floating-point numbers. For critical operations involving high precision, consider using the **decimal** module in Python.

Overall, understanding how to work with integers and floating-point numbers is essential for performing mathematical calculations and writing numerical algorithms in Python.

CHAPTER 7

BOOLEAN DATA TYPE

The Boolean data type in Python represents a binary value, which can have one of two states: **True** or **False**. Booleans are commonly used to represent the truth values of logical expressions. In Python, the Boolean data type is represented using the **bool** class. Let's explore some aspects of the Boolean data type:

Creating Boolean Variables: You can create Boolean variables by directly assigning the values **True** or **False** to them.

```
is_raining = True

is_sunny = False
```

Boolean Expressions: Boolean expressions are logical expressions that evaluate to either True or False. These expressions often involve comparison operators (e.g., ==, !=, <, >, <=, >=) and logical operators (e.g., and, or, not).

```
x = 5

y = 10

# Comparison

is_equal = x == y        # False

is_not_equal = x != y    # True
```

```
is_greater = x > y        # False
is_less = x < y           # True
is_greater_or_equal = x >= y  # False
is_less_or_equal = x <= y     # True
# Logical
is_both_true = is_raining and is_sunny  # False
is_either_true = is_raining or is_sunny  # True
is_not_true = not is_raining            # False
```

Boolean Conversions: In Python, several data types can be implicitly converted to Booleans. Any non-zero numeric value or non-empty sequence or container is considered True, while zero, None, and empty sequences or containers are considered False.

```
# Numeric conversions
bool(10)     # True
bool(0)      # False
# Sequence conversions
bool("hello")   # True
bool("")        # False
# Container conversions
bool([1, 2, 3])  # True
```

```
bool([])        # False
```

Boolean in Control Structures: Boolean values are widely used in control structures like **if**, **while**, and **for** loops to conditionally execute code blocks.

```
# Example with if statement
temperature = 25
if temperature > 30:
  print("It's hot!")
else:
  print("It's not hot.")
# Example with while loop
count = 0
while count < 5:
  print("Hello")
  count += 1
```

Booleans are fundamental for decision-making and controlling the flow of your Python programs. They play a vital role in creating conditional statements, loops, and other logic-based operations.

CHAPTER 8
WORKING WITH LISTS

Working with lists is a fundamental aspect of Python programming. Lists are ordered collections of elements that can be of different data types. They are mutable, meaning you can modify the elements after the list is created. Here are some common operations and techniques for working with lists:

Creating Lists: You can create a list by enclosing elements in square brackets **[]**.

```
numbers = [1, 2, 3, 4, 5]

fruits = ["apple", "banana", "orange"]

mixed_list = [1, "hello", True, 3.14]
```

Accessing Elements: You can access individual elements in a list using indexing. Python uses zero-based indexing.

```
fruits = ["apple", "banana", "orange"]

print(fruits[0])    # Output: 'apple'

print(fruits[1])    # Output: 'banana'

print(fruits[-1])    # Output: 'orange' (negative index starts from the end)
```

Slicing Lists: You can extract a sublist (slice) from a list using slicing.

```
numbers = [1, 2, 3, 4, 5]
print(numbers[1:4])   # Output: [2, 3, 4]
print(numbers[:3])    # Output: [1, 2, 3]
print(numbers[2:])    # Output: [3, 4, 5]
```

Modifying Lists: Lists are mutable, so you can modify their elements or extend them.

```
fruits = ["apple", "banana", "orange"]
fruits[0] = "grape"  # Modifying an element
fruits.append("kiwi") # Adding an element to the end
fruits.insert(1, "mango")  # Inserting an element at a specific position
```

List Comprehensions: List comprehensions provide a concise way to create lists based on existing lists or other iterable objects.

```
# Example: Create a list of squares
numbers = [1, 2, 3, 4, 5]
squares = [num ** 2 for num in numbers]
print(squares)  # Output: [1, 4, 9, 16, 25]
```

Other List Methods: Python provides a range of built-in methods for working with lists, such as remove(), pop(), extend(), count(), index(), sort(), and more.

```
numbers = [1, 2, 3, 4, 3]

numbers.remove(3)  # Remove the first occurrence of 3

numbers.pop()      # Remove and return the last element

numbers.extend([5, 6])  # Add elements from another list to the
end

count_of_3 = numbers.count(3)  # Count the occurrences of 3

index_of_2 = numbers.index(2)  # Find the index of 2 in the list

numbers.sort()     # Sort the list in ascending order
```

Copying Lists: Be careful when copying lists. Assignment (=) creates a reference to the original list, meaning changes in one list will affect the other. To create an independent copy, use slicing or the copy() method.

```
numbers = [1, 2, 3, 4, 5]

# Creating a shallow copy using slicing

numbers_copy = numbers[:]

# Creating a shallow copy using the copy() method

numbers_copy = numbers.copy()
```

Working with lists is essential for various data processing tasks and algorithms. Mastering list manipulation will make you more proficient in Python programming.

Understanding Tuples

Tuples are another built-in data type in Python that are similar to lists but with some key differences. Like lists, tuples are ordered collections of elements, but unlike lists, tuples are immutable, meaning their elements cannot be changed after creation. Tuples are represented using parentheses () instead of square brackets []. Here are some important characteristics of tuples:

Creating Tuples:

You can create a tuple by enclosing elements in parentheses ().

```
my_tuple = (1, 2, 3)

fruits = ("apple", "banana", "orange")

mixed_tuple = (1, "hello", True, 3.14)
```

Accessing Elements:

You can access individual elements in a tuple using indexing, just like with lists.

```
my_tuple = (1, 2, 3, 4, 5)

print(my_tuple[0])  # Output: 1

print(my_tuple[2])  # Output: 3
```

print(my_tuple[-1]) # Output: 5 (negative index starts from the end)

Tuples are Immutable:

Once a tuple is created, you cannot modify its elements or extend it with additional elements.

my_tuple = (1, 2, 3)

my_tuple[0] = 10   # This will raise an error since tuples are immutable

Advantages of Tuples:

Use tuples when you want to ensure that the data remains constant and unchanged throughout the program.

Tuples are more memory-efficient than lists because they are immutable. Once a tuple is created, the memory allocated for it cannot change, unlike lists that may dynamically resize.

Tuples vs. Lists:

Choose between tuples and lists based on your specific use case:

Use tuples when you have a fixed set of elements and you don't want the data to be changed accidentally.

Use lists when you need a dynamic collection of elements and need to modify, extend, or reorder the data.

Tuple Packing and Unpacking:

Tuple packing is the process of creating a tuple by placing multiple comma-separated values inside parentheses. Tuple unpacking allows you to assign the elements of a tuple to individual variables.

```
# Tuple packing
coordinates = 10, 20
print(coordinates)  # Output: (10, 20)
# Tuple unpacking
x, y = coordinates
print(x)  # Output: 10
print(y)  # Output: 20
```

Tuples in Function Return:

Tuples are often used to return multiple values from a function.

```
def get_coordinates():
  x = 10
  y = 20
  return x, y
# Tuple unpacking to receive multiple return values
x, y = get_coordinates()
```

Tuples are a useful data structure when you need to ensure the immutability of a collection or return multiple values from a function. They complement lists in Python and provide more options for managing and representing data.

Using Dictionaries

Dictionaries are another important data structure in Python. They are unordered collections of key-value pairs, where each key is unique and associated with a value. Dictionaries are also known as associative arrays, hash maps, or hash tables in other programming languages. Here are some key features and operations related to dictionaries:

Creating Dictionaries:

You can create a dictionary by enclosing key-value pairs in curly braces {}.

```
person = {
  "name": "John Doe",
  "age": 30,
  "email": "john.doe@example.com"
}
fruits = {
  "apple": 1.0,
```

```
  "banana": 1.5,
  "orange": 0.8
}
```

Accessing Values:

You can access the values in a dictionary using the corresponding keys.

```
print(person["name"])     # Output: 'John Doe'
print(fruits["banana"])   # Output: 1.5
```

Modifying and Adding Key-Value Pairs:

Dictionaries are mutable, so you can modify existing values or add new key-value pairs.

```
person["age"] = 35       # Modifying the 'age' value
person["city"] = "New York"  # Adding a new key-value pair
```

Dictionary Methods:

Python provides various built-in methods for working with dictionaries.

```
fruits = {
  "apple": 1.0,
  "banana": 1.5,
  "orange": 0.8
```

```
}
# Get all keys and values
keys = fruits.keys()        # Output: dict_keys(['apple', 'banana', 'orange'])
values = fruits.values()    # Output: dict_values([1.0, 1.5, 0.8])
# Check if a key exists
if "apple" in fruits:
  print("Apple is in the dictionary.")
```

Iterating through a Dictionary:

You can use loops to iterate through the keys, values, or key-value pairs of a dictionary.

```
fruits = {
  "apple": 1.0,
  "banana": 1.5,
  "orange": 0.8
}
# Iterate through keys
for key in fruits:
  print(key)
# Iterate through values
```

```
for value in fruits.values():
  print(value)
# Iterate through key-value pairs
for key, value in fruits.items():
  print(key, value)
```

Nested Dictionaries:

Dictionaries can be nested inside each other, allowing you to create complex data structures.

```
students = {
  "John": {
    "age": 25,
    "grades": [85, 90, 78]
  },
  "Alice": {
    "age": 23,
    "grades": [95, 92, 88]
  }
}
```

Dictionaries are useful for representing structured data with associated values. They are widely used for various tasks, such as storing configurations, organizing data, and solving algorithmic problems. Understanding dictionaries will enhance your ability to work with more complex data in Python.

CHAPTER 9

CONDITIONALS AND LOOPS

Comparison Operators

Comparison operators in Python are used to compare two values and return a Boolean value (True or False) based on the comparison result. These operators allow you to check relationships between variables or values. Here are the common comparison operators in Python:

1. Equal To: ==

Checks if the left and right operands are equal.

Returns True if they are equal; otherwise, returns False.

```
x = 10
y = 5
result = x == y
print(result)  # Output: False
```

2. Not Equal To: !=

Checks if the left and right operands are not equal.

Returns True if they are not equal; otherwise, returns False.

```
x = 10
```

```
y = 5

result = x != y

print(result)  # Output: True
```

3. Greater Than: >

Checks if the left operand is greater than the right operand.

Returns True if the left operand is greater; otherwise, returns False.

```
x = 10

y = 5

result = x > y

print(result)  # Output: True
```

4. Less Than: <

Checks if the left operand is less than the right operand.

Returns True if the left operand is less; otherwise, returns False.

```
x = 10

y = 5

result = x < y

print(result)  # Output: False
```

5. Greater Than or Equal To: >=

Checks if the left operand is greater than or equal to the right operand.

Returns True if the left operand is greater than or equal; otherwise, returns False.

```
x = 10

y = 5

result = x >= y

print(result)  # Output: True
```

6. Less Than or Equal To: <=

Checks if the left operand is less than or equal to the right operand.

Returns True if the left operand is less than or equal; otherwise, returns False.

```
x = 10

y = 5

result = x <= y

print(result)  # Output: False
```

Comparison operators are widely used in conditional statements (e.g., if, while) and are essential for decision-making and logic control in Python programs. They allow you to compare values and take actions based on the comparison results.

If-Else Conditional Statements

If-else conditional statements are a fundamental part of programming in Python. They allow you to make decisions based on conditions, executing specific blocks of code if certain conditions are met. The syntax of an if-else statement is as follows:

```
if condition:
  # Code block to be executed if the condition is True
else:
  # Code block to be executed if the condition is False
```

Example:

```
x = 10
if x > 5:
  print("x is greater than 5")
else:
  print("x is not greater than 5")
```

In this example, if the value of x is greater than 5, the statement within the if block will be executed, and if x is not greater than 5, the statement within the else block will be executed.

Nested If-Else Statements:

You can also use nested if-else statements to handle more complex conditions. Here's an example:

```python
x = 10
if x > 5:
    print("x is greater than 5")
elif x == 5:
    print("x is equal to 5")
else:
    print("x is less than 5")
```

In this case, if x is greater than 5, the first block will be executed. If x is equal to 5, the second block will be executed. If both conditions are false, the code in the else block will be executed.

Chained Conditional Operators:

You can also use chained conditional operators (and, or) to combine multiple conditions in an if-else statement.

```python
x = 10
y = 20
if x > 5 and y > 15:
    print("Both x and y meet the conditions")
else:
    print("Either x or y does not meet the conditions")
```

In this example, the and operator checks if both conditions (x > 5 and y > 15) are True for the if block to be executed.

Multiple Elif Statements:

You can have multiple elif statements to handle more cases in your if-else logic.

```
x = 0

if x > 0:

  print("x is positive")

elif x < 0:

  print("x is negative")

else:

  print("x is zero")
```

In this case, if x is positive, the first block will be executed. If x is negative, the second block will be executed. If both conditions are false, the code in the else block will be executed.

Conditional statements are powerful tools for controlling the flow of your program based on different conditions. They allow your code to adapt and make decisions dynamically, improving the flexibility and functionality of your Python programs.

For Loops and While Loops

For Loops:

For loops in Python are used to iterate over elements in a sequence (such as a list, tuple, string, or dictionary) or any other iterable object. The basic syntax of a for loop is as follows:

```
for element in sequence:
    # Code block to be executed for each element
```

Example:

```
fruits = ["apple", "banana", "orange"]
for fruit in fruits:
    print(fruit)
```

In this example, the for loop iterates over each element in the fruits list and prints each fruit on a new line.

Range() Function:

The range() function is often used with for loops to generate a sequence of numbers. It can take one, two, or three arguments, similar to the range() function in loops in many other programming languages.

```
for i in range(5):
    print(i)
```

In this example, the for loop iterates five times, with i taking values from 0 to 4.

Nested For Loops:

You can have nested for loops, allowing you to iterate over multiple sequences simultaneously.

```
adj = ["red", "big", "tasty"]
fruits = ["apple", "banana", "cherry"]
for a in adj:
  for f in fruits:
    print(a, f)
```

This nested loop will generate all possible combinations of adjectives and fruits.

While Loops:

While loops in Python are used to repeatedly execute a block of code as long as a specified condition is True. The basic syntax of a while loop is as follows:

```
while condition:
  # Code block to be executed while the condition is True
```

Example:

```
count = 0
while count < 5:
  print("Hello")
  count += 1
```

In this example, the while loop will print "Hello" five times.

Break and Continue Statements:

You can use break and continue statements inside loops to control the loop's behavior. The break statement is used to exit the loop prematurely, while the continue statement is used to skip the current iteration and move to the next one.

Example:

```
for i in range(10):
 if i == 3:
    continue
 if i == 7:
    break
 print(i)
```

In this example, the loop will print numbers from 0 to 6 but will skip printing 3 and exit the loop when i becomes 7.

Both for loops and while loops are essential for performing repetitive tasks, iterating over collections, and implementing algorithms that require repeated execution. They are fundamental tools for controlling the flow of your Python programs.

Break and Continue Statements

The break statement in Python is used to terminate the execution of a loop prematurely. When the break statement is encountered within a loop, the loop is immediately exited, and the program continues with the first statement after the loop.

Example:

```
for i in range(5):
    if i == 3:
        break
    print(i)
```

In this example, the loop will print numbers from 0 to 2 and then encounter the break statement when i becomes 3. As a result, the loop terminates immediately, and the program continues with the first statement after the loop.

Continue Statement:

The continue statement in Python is used to skip the current iteration of a loop and move to the next iteration. When the continue statement is encountered within a loop, the rest of the code block for that iteration is skipped, and the loop proceeds with the next iteration.

Example:

```
for i in range(5):
```

```
    if i == 2:
        continue
    print(i)
```

In this example, the loop will print numbers from 0 to 4 but will skip printing 2 because the continue statement is encountered when i is 2. The loop proceeds to the next iteration, and the value 2 is not printed.

Using Break and Continue in Loops:

Both break and continue statements are often used within loops to control the flow of the loop based on specific conditions. For example, you might use the break statement to exit a loop early if a certain condition is met or use the continue statement to skip over specific elements in an iteration.

Example with Break:

```
# Find the first occurrence of a target element in a list
target = 5
numbers = [1, 2, 5, 4, 5, 3, 6]
for num in numbers:
    if num == target:
        print(f"Found {target}!")
        break
```

In this example, the loop will search for the first occurrence of target (which is 5) in the numbers list. When it finds the first 5, it prints the message and exits the loop using the break statement.

Example with Continue:

```
# Print only even numbers from a list
numbers = [1, 2, 3, 4, 5, 6, 7, 8, 9]
for num in numbers:
  if num % 2 != 0:
    continue
  print(num)
```

In this example, the loop iterates through the numbers list and uses the continue statement to skip odd numbers. Only even numbers are printed in the output.

Both break and continue statements are powerful tools for fine-tuning the behavior of loops and making your code more efficient and flexible.

Defining Functions

Defining functions in Python allows you to create reusable blocks of code that can be executed whenever needed. Functions help in organizing your code, improving readability, and promoting code reusability. Here's the basic syntax to define a function in Python:

```
def function_name(parameters):
  # Code block for the function
  # You can use the parameters within the function
  # Optionally, return a value using the 'return' statement
```

Let's break down the components:

def: This keyword is used to define a function in Python.

function_name: Choose a descriptive name for your function that follows Python's naming conventions. The function name should be lowercase, and if it has multiple words, separate them with underscores (snake_case).

parameters: These are optional. If your function needs input data to work with, you can define parameters inside the parentheses. Multiple parameters can be separated by commas.

Code Block: The indented code inside the function is the function's body, which contains the logic to be executed when the function is called.

return: This keyword is optional but is used to specify the value that the function should return. If the return statement is omitted, the function returns None by default.

Example:

```
def greet(name):
  return f"Hello, {name}!"
result = greet("John")
print(result)  # Output: "Hello, John!"
```

In this example, we defined a function called greet that takes one parameter name. When the function is called with the argument "John", it returns the greeting message, which is then printed.

Calling Functions:

To execute a function and run the code inside it, you simply call the function by its name and provide any required arguments within the parentheses.

```
def say_hello():
  print("Hello!")
# Call the function
say_hello()  # Output: "Hello!"
```

Default Parameters:

You can also provide default values to parameters, making them optional when calling the function.

```
def greet(name="Guest"):
```

```
    return f"Hello, {name}!"
result1 = greet()      # Output: "Hello, Guest!"
result2 = greet("John") # Output: "Hello, John!"
```

In this example, the name parameter has a default value of "Guest". If no argument is provided when calling the function, it uses the default value.

Variable Number of Arguments:

Python functions can receive a variable number of arguments using the *args and **kwargs syntax. *args allows you to pass a variable number of non-keyword arguments, while **kwargs allows you to pass a variable number of keyword arguments.

Example:

```
def sum_all(*args):
    total = 0
    for num in args:
        total += num
    return total
result = sum_all(1, 2, 3, 4, 5)
print(result)  # Output: 15
```

In this example, the sum_all function can accept any number of arguments, and it calculates the sum of all the arguments passed.

Defining functions in Python allows you to encapsulate logic, promote reusability, and make your code more organized and maintainable. Use functions to break down complex tasks into smaller, manageable units, and call them whenever you need to perform the corresponding operations.

Function Parameters and Arguments

Function parameters and arguments are essential concepts in Python that allow you to pass data into a function when it is called. Parameters are the variables defined in the function definition, while arguments are the actual values passed to the function when calling it.

Function Parameters:

Parameters are the placeholders for the values that a function expects to receive when it is called. They are listed inside the parentheses in the function definition.

Syntax:

```
def function_name(parameter1, parameter2, ...):
  # Function code that uses the parameters
```

Example:

```
def greet(name):
  print(f"Hello, {name}!")
```

```
greet("John")  # "name" is the parameter with the value "John"
greet("Alice") # "name" is the parameter with the value "Alice"
```

In this example, the greet function takes a single parameter name, and the function code uses the value of the name parameter to print the greeting message.

Function Arguments:

Arguments are the actual values that are passed to a function when it is called. They correspond to the function's parameters and are enclosed in the parentheses at the time of calling the function.

Syntax:

```
function_name(argument1, argument2, ...)
```

Example:

```
def add_numbers(x, y):
  return x + y
result = add_numbers(3, 5)  # 3 and 5 are the arguments for x and y, respectively
print(result)  # Output: 8
```

In this example, the add_numbers function takes two parameters x and y. When we call the function with add_numbers(3, 5), the values 3 and 5 are the arguments for x and y, respectively.

Default Parameters:

You can provide default values to function parameters, making them optional when calling the function. If an argument is not passed for a parameter with a default value, the default value will be used.

Syntax:

```
def function_name(parameter1=default_value1, parameter2=default_value2, ...):
  # Function code that uses the parameters
```

Example:

```
def greet(name="Guest"):
  print(f"Hello, {name}!")
greet()       # Uses the default value "Guest"
greet("John") # Uses the argument "John" for the "name" parameter
```

In this example, the greet function has a default parameter value of "Guest" for the name parameter. When called without an argument, it uses the default value.

Function parameters and arguments are essential for passing data into functions and enabling the reuse of code with different input values. By using parameters, functions can be made more flexible and versatile, making them a crucial aspect of Python programming.

Default Values and Scope

Default values in Python allow you to define default values for function parameters. If an argument is not provided for a parameter with a default value, the function will use the default value during the function call. Default values provide flexibility and allow functions to work even if some arguments are not passed.

Example:

```
def greet(name="Guest"):
  print(f"Hello, {name}!")
greet()        # Output: "Hello, Guest!"
greet("John")  # Output: "Hello, John!"
```

In this example, the greet function has a default parameter value of "Guest" for the name parameter. When the function is called without an argument, it uses the default value and greets the guest. When an argument is provided (e.g., "John"), it uses the provided argument to greet the person.

Scope:

Scope in Python refers to the region in which a variable is accessible. There are two main types of scope in Python:

Global Scope: Variables defined outside any function or block have a global scope. They can be accessed from any part of the code, including inside functions.

Example:

```
x = 10  # Global variable
def print_x():
  print(x)  # Accessing global variable inside the function
print_x()  # Output: 10
```

In this example, the variable x is defined outside the function print_x, so it has global scope and can be accessed inside the function.

Local Scope: Variables defined inside a function have a local scope and are accessible only within that function.

Example:

```
def print_number():
  y = 20  # Local variable
  print(y)
print_number()  # Output: 20
# The following line will raise an error since "y" is not defined outside the function
# print(y)
```

In this example, the variable y is defined inside the function print_number, so it has a local scope and cannot be accessed outside the function.

It's important to note that the scope of a variable determines its visibility and lifetime. Variables with local scope are created when the function is called and destroyed when the function finishes execution. On the other hand, variables with global scope are created when the program starts and persist until the program ends.

Global Keyword:

To modify a global variable inside a function, you need to use the global keyword to declare that you want to use the global variable instead of creating a local one.

Example:

```
x = 10

def increment_x():

  global x

  x += 1

increment_x()

print(x)  # Output: 11
```

In this example, the global keyword is used inside the increment_x function to indicate that we want to modify the global variable x instead of creating a local variable with the same name.

Understanding default values and variable scope is essential for writing functions that are flexible, reusable, and maintainable.

Properly defining and using variable scope helps prevent naming conflicts and ensures that your code works as intended.

Introduction to Modules

In Python, a module is a file that contains Python definitions, statements, and functions. Modules are used to organize code into separate files, making it easier to manage and reuse code across different projects. Each module can contain variables, functions, and classes that can be imported and used in other Python scripts or modules.

Modules offer the following advantages:

Code Reusability: Modules allow you to write code once and reuse it in multiple programs, making it easier to maintain and update shared functionalities.

Organized Codebase: By breaking down your code into smaller modules, you can organize and structure your project, improving code readability and maintainability.

Avoiding Naming Conflicts: Modules provide a namespace for variables and functions, helping to avoid naming conflicts when multiple modules use similar variable names.

Encapsulation: Modules help in encapsulating related code into separate units, promoting better separation of concerns.

Python comes with a standard library that includes a vast collection of modules for various purposes, such as math operations, file handling, network communication, and more. You can also create your own custom modules to organize your code.

Creating a Module:

To create a module, simply save your Python code in a .py file with the desired module name. For example, if you want to create a module called my_module, you can save the code in a file named my_module.py.

Example:

my_module.py:

```
def add(a, b):
 return a + b
def multiply(a, b):
 return a * b
pi = 3.14159
```

Using a Module:

To use functions and variables from a module, you need to import the module into your Python script. You can use the import statement for this purpose.

Example:

main.py:

```
import my_module

result_sum = my_module.add(5, 3)

print(result_sum)  # Output: 8

result_mult = my_module.multiply(2, 4)

print(result_mult)  # Output: 8

print(my_module.pi)  # Output: 3.14159
```

In this example, we imported the my_module module into the main.py script and used its functions add() and multiply(), as well as the variable pi.

Importing Specific Functions or Variables:

If you only need specific functions or variables from a module, you can import them directly using the from statement.

Example:

```
from my_module import add, multiply, pi

result_sum = add(5, 3)

print(result_sum)  # Output: 8

result_mult = multiply(2, 4)

print(result_mult)  # Output: 8

print(pi)  # Output: 3.14159
```

In this example, we imported only the add(), multiply(), and pi from the my_module module, making them directly accessible in the script without the need to prefix them with the module name.

Modules are a powerful feature in Python that allows you to organize and share code effectively. They help in creating more maintainable and scalable projects by promoting code reusability and modular design.

Built-in Functions and String Functions

Python comes with a rich set of built-in functions that are readily available for use without the need for additional imports. These functions perform common operations and tasks and make Python a powerful and versatile programming language. Here are some essential built-in functions:

1. **print()**: Used to display output to the console.
2. **input(prompt)**: Used to take user input from the console.
3. **len(iterable)**: Returns the number of elements in an iterable (e.g., string, list, tuple).
4. **range(start, stop[, step])**: Generates a sequence of numbers from **start** to **stop - 1**, with an optional **step** value.
5. **type(obj)**: Returns the type of an object (e.g., int, float, str, list).
6. **max(iterable)**: Returns the largest element from an iterable.

7. **min(iterable)**: Returns the smallest element from an iterable.

8. **sum(iterable)**: Returns the sum of all elements in an iterable.

9. **abs(x)**: Returns the absolute value of a number.

10. **round(number[, ndigits])**: Rounds a number to the nearest integer or to the specified number of decimal places.

String Functions:

In addition to the built-in functions, Python also provides various built-in string methods that can be used to manipulate strings. Strings in Python are sequences of characters and support a wide range of operations and manipulations. Here are some commonly used string methods:

1. **str.upper()**: Converts all characters in the string to uppercase.

2. **str.lower()**: Converts all characters in the string to lowercase.

3. **str.capitalize()**: Capitalizes the first character of the string.

4. **str.title()**: Capitalizes the first character of each word in the string.

5. **str.strip([characters])**: Removes leading and trailing whitespace (or specified characters) from the string.

6. **str.split([separator])**: Splits the string into a list of substrings based on the specified separator.

7. **str.join(iterable)**: Joins the elements of an iterable into a single string using the string as a separator.

8. **str.replace(old, new)**: Replaces occurrences of a substring with a new substring.

9. **str.startswith(prefix)**: Returns True if the string starts with the specified prefix.

10. **str.endswith(suffix)**: Returns True if the string ends with the specified suffix.

These are just a few examples of built-in functions and string methods available in Python. There are many more functions and methods provided by Python's standard library that you can explore and use for various tasks in your programs. To discover more built-in functions and string methods, you can refer to Python's official documentation.

CHAPTER 10

EXCEPTION HANDLING

Try and Except Blocks

Try and Except blocks, also known as try-except blocks, are used in Python for handling exceptions and preventing your program from crashing when an error occurs. They provide a way to gracefully handle exceptions and take appropriate actions instead of halting the program abruptly.

Syntax:

```
try:
  # Code that may raise an exception
  # ...
except ExceptionType:
  # Code to handle the exception
  # ...
```

How it Works:

The code inside the try block is the part where you want to execute some operations that might raise an exception.

If an exception occurs within the try block, the code execution jumps to the corresponding except block.

The except block contains the code that handles the specific type of exception you expect to encounter.

Example:

Let's see a simple example of try-except block:

```
try:
  num1 = int(input("Enter a number: "))
  num2 = int(input("Enter another number: "))
  result = num1 / num2
  print(f"The result of the division is: {result}")
except ValueError:
  print("Invalid input. Please enter valid integers.")
except ZeroDivisionError:
  print("Error: Cannot divide by zero.")
```

In this example, we are trying to take two numbers as input, perform division, and print the result. However, if the user provides invalid input (non-integer) or attempts to divide by zero, an exception will be raised. The corresponding except blocks will handle these exceptions gracefully and display appropriate error messages.

Using Generic Except Block:

You can also use a generic except block to catch any type of exception:

```
try:
    # Code that may raise an exception
    # ...
except:
    # Code to handle the exception
    # ...
```

While using a generic except block is convenient, it is generally considered better practice to catch specific exceptions whenever possible. This allows you to handle different types of errors differently and provides better debugging information.

Handling Multiple Exceptions:

You can also handle multiple types of exceptions within the same try-except block:

```
try:
    # Code that may raise an exception
    # ...
except (ExceptionType1, ExceptionType2):
```

```
    # Code to handle the exceptions
    # ...
```

This way, you can handle different exception types with the same block of code.

Using else and finally:

else: You can use the else block after the except block to specify code that should be executed if no exception occurs in the try block.

```
try:
    # Code that may raise an exception
    # ...
except ExceptionType:
    # Code to handle the exception
    # ...
else:
    # Code to execute if no exception occurs
    # ...
```

finally: The finally block is used to specify cleanup code that should always be executed, regardless of whether an exception occurred or not.

```
try:
```

```
    # Code that may raise an exception
    # ...
except ExceptionType:
    # Code to handle the exception
    # ...
finally:
    # Cleanup code (always executed)
    # ...
```

Using try-except blocks helps in writing robust and error-tolerant code, ensuring that your program handles unexpected situations gracefully without crashing. It is particularly useful when dealing with user inputs or external data that may not always be in the expected format.

Handling Different Types of Errors

Handling different types of errors is essential to provide specific and meaningful responses when exceptions occur in your Python programs. Instead of catching all exceptions using a generic except block, you can use multiple except blocks to handle various types of errors differently. This allows you to respond appropriately to different situations and provide useful feedback to users or loggers.

Syntax:

```
try:
  # Code that may raise an exception
  # ...
except ExceptionType1:
  # Code to handle the first type of exception
  # ...
except ExceptionType2:
  # Code to handle the second type of exception
  # ...
# Add more except blocks for handling other types of exceptions
```

Example:

Let's see an example of handling different types of errors:

```
try:
  num1 = int(input("Enter a number: "))
  num2 = int(input("Enter another number: "))
  result = num1 / num2
  print(f"The result of the division is: {result}")
except ValueError:
  print("Invalid input. Please enter valid integers.")
```

```
except ZeroDivisionError:
    print("Error: Cannot divide by zero.")
except Exception as e:
    print(f"An error occurred: {e}")
```

In this example, we use three different except blocks:

The first block catches ValueError when the user provides non-integer input.

The second block catches ZeroDivisionError when the user tries to divide by zero.

The third block is a generic exception handler that catches any other type of exception and displays the error message.

Using multiple except blocks allows you to customize the error handling for specific scenarios. It also helps you to pinpoint the specific issue and take appropriate actions accordingly.

Handling Multiple Exceptions with One Block:

If you want to handle multiple types of exceptions in the same way, you can group them together in one except block:

```
try:
    # Code that may raise an exception
    # ...
except (ExceptionType1, ExceptionType2):
```

```
    # Code to handle these types of exceptions
    # ...
```

Handling Exceptions in a Loop:

When working with loops, you might want to continue the loop even if an exception occurs. You can achieve this by placing the try-except block inside the loop:

```
while True:
  try:
    num = int(input("Enter a number: "))
    print(f"The square of the number is: {num * num}")
  except ValueError:
    print("Invalid input. Please enter a valid number.")
```

In this example, if the user enters an invalid input (non-integer), the program displays an error message and continues with the next iteration of the loop.

By handling different types of errors appropriately, you can make your code more robust and user-friendly, preventing crashes and providing clear feedback when things go wrong.

Advance tips and tricks

1. List Comprehensions for Concise Code:

Instead of traditional loops, leverage list comprehensions for succinct and expressive creation of lists. For example, **squares = [x**2 for x in range(10)]**.

2. Dictionary Comprehensions:

Similar to list comprehensions, use dictionary comprehensions to create dictionaries efficiently, such as **squares_dict = {x: x**2 for x in range(10)}**.

3. Generator Expressions for Memory Efficiency:

When working with large datasets, consider using generator expressions to produce values on-the-fly, conserving memory. For instance, **squares_gen = (x**2 for x in range(10))**.

4. Multiple Assignments in One Line:

Python allows multiple assignments in a single line, making the code more concise. For instance, **a, b, c = 1, 2, 3**.

5. Unpacking in Function Arguments:

Utilize the * operator for unpacking iterables when passing arguments to a function. For example, **print(*numbers)** is equivalent to **print(1, 2, 3)** where **numbers = [1, 2, 3]**.

6. Underscore (_) for Ignoring Values:

Use the underscore (_) as a variable name to indicate that a value is intentionally ignored. For example, **_, second_value, _ = get_values()**.

7. Decorators for Code Reusability:

Decorators allow you to modify or extend the behavior of functions, enhancing code reuse. They can be used for tasks like logging, timing, or authentication.

8. Context Managers with with Statement:

Employ context managers with the **with** statement for resource management. This is particularly useful for working with files, databases, or network connections.

9. Use collections Module for Specialized Data Structures:

Leverage the **collections** module for specialized data structures like **defaultdict**, **Counter**, and **namedtuple**. For instance, **frequency = defaultdict(int)**.

10. Concurrency with asyncio:

For asynchronous programming, use the **asyncio** module to write asynchronous code. This is especially beneficial for I/O-bound tasks.

11. Type Annotations and Type Hints:

Enhance code readability and catch potential errors early by incorporating type annotations and type hints, such as **def greeting(name: str) -> str**.

12. Functional Programming with functools Module:

The **functools** module provides higher-order functions and operations on callable objects. For example, using **reduce** for multiplication: **product = reduce((lambda x, y: x * y), [1, 2, 3, 4])**.

These advanced tips and tricks are tools in your Python toolbox. Experiment with them, adopt those that fit your style and needs, and elevate your Python programming to new heights.

Future of python

As of early 2023, Python continues to be one of the most popular and widely used programming languages. Its versatility, readability, and extensive ecosystem contribute to its sustained growth and relevance. Here are some aspects that indicate a promising future for Python:

1. **AI and Machine Learning:** Python has become the language of choice for many AI and machine learning practitioners. Frameworks like TensorFlow, PyTorch, and scikit-learn are widely adopted, solidifying Python's position in the rapidly expanding field of artificial intelligence.

2. **Data Science and Analytics:** Python remains a dominant force in the field of data science and analytics. Libraries such as pandas, NumPy, and Matplotlib are instrumental in data manipulation, analysis, and visualization.

3. **Web Development and Frameworks:** Python web frameworks like Django and Flask continue to gain popularity,

offering developers powerful tools for building scalable and maintainable web applications. Python's simplicity and readability make it an attractive choice for web development.

4. **Automation and Scripting:** Python's ease of use makes it a preferred language for automation and scripting. Its applications extend to various domains, from system administration tasks to network programming.

5. **Education and Community:** Python's readability and simplicity make it an excellent choice for teaching programming. It has a large and active community that contributes to its growth, development, and the creation of extensive documentation and resources.

6. **Containerization and DevOps:** Python is widely used in DevOps practices and the containerization ecosystem. Tools like Ansible, Docker, and Kubernetes have Python bindings and APIs, facilitating automation and orchestration in modern infrastructure.

7. **Cross-Platform Development:** Python's compatibility across different operating systems and platforms enhances its appeal. This makes it a strong candidate for cross-platform development, contributing to its adoption in various application domains.

8. **Serverless Computing:** Python is well-suited for serverless computing models. Platforms like AWS Lambda and Azure

Functions support Python, enabling developers to build and deploy serverless applications seamlessly.

9. **Community and Open Source Contributions:** Python's open-source nature encourages community collaboration and contributions. This collaborative spirit ensures continuous improvement, bug fixes, and the development of new features.

It's essential to stay updated with the latest trends and developments in the Python ecosystem. As technology evolves, Python is likely to adapt and remain a prominent player in various domains. As of the last update, Python's future appears bright, driven by its versatility and the ongoing contributions of the global developer community.

CONCLUSION

As we draw the curtains on this journey through the intricacies and wonders of Python, it's not merely the conclusion of a book but an invitation to a vast and ever-expanding realm of possibilities. "Python for Beginners" has been your guide, unveiling the beauty and versatility of a language that has become more than just a tool; it's a community, an ecosystem, and a gateway to the future.

Reflecting on the Python Odyssey:

From the introductory chapters that eased you into the syntax, to the advanced tips and tricks that empowered you to write efficient and elegant code, this book has been a companion on your Pythonic odyssey. Together, we've explored the foundations—variables, loops, functions—and ventured into the realm of decorators, context managers, and asynchronous programming.

Python's Impact on Diverse Domains:

Python's influence extends far beyond its syntax. It's a force in artificial intelligence, machine learning, data science, web development, and beyond. Its adaptability and readability have made it a favorite for beginners and seasoned developers alike. The success stories of Python in real-world applications, from startups to large enterprises, affirm its relevance across diverse domains.

The Pythonic Community:

One of Python's greatest strengths lies in its community—a global collective of enthusiasts, educators, and contributors. The collaborative spirit of open source, the countless libraries and frameworks, and the willingness to share knowledge define the Pythonic ethos. As you conclude this book, remember that your journey doesn't end here; it transforms into an ongoing exploration within this thriving community.

Python and the Future:

The future of Python appears dynamic and promising. With continual advancements in AI, data science, and web development, Python is poised to play a pivotal role. Its simplicity, readability, and extensive libraries position it as a language that adapts to emerging technologies and remains at the forefront of innovation.

Embracing Lifelong Learning:

As you venture beyond these pages, embrace the spirit of lifelong learning. Python is a tool, a companion, and a skill that evolves with you. Stay curious, explore new libraries, contribute to open source, and, above all, continue to code. Your Python journey is a perpetual expedition, and each line of code you write is a step toward mastery.

Gratitude and Encouragement:

Thank you for choosing "Python for Beginners" as your guide. Whether you're a student embarking on your coding journey, a professional expanding your skill set, or simply an enthusiast passionate about the art of programming, your dedication to learning Python is commendable. As you face new challenges, may the principles and insights gained within these pages serve as a steadfast companion.

So, as this chapter concludes, remember: your Python journey is not finite; it's a continuum. Here's to the code you've written, the challenges you've overcome, and the boundless possibilities that await you in the expansive world of Python. Happy coding, and may your future endeavors be as exciting and rewarding as your journey with Python has been!